REA

ACPL ITEM
DISCARDED

S0-BKV-614

DISPLAY BOARDS

The Instructional Media Library

Volume Number 3

DISPLAY BOARDS

Robert V. Bullough, Sr.
Educational Systems and Learning Resources
University of Utah

James E. Duane
Series Editor

Educational Technology Publications
Englewood Cliffs, New Jersey 07632

ALLEN COUNTY PUBLIC LIBRARY
FORT WAYNE, INDIANA

Library of Congress Cataloging in Publication Data

Bullough, Robert V
    Display boards.

        (The Instructional media library ; v. no. 3)
        Bibliography: p.
        1. Display boards. 2. Displays in education.
    I. Title. II. Series: Instructional media library ;
    v. no. 3.
    LB1043.6.B84   371.3'356   80-21332
    ISBN 0-87778-163-X

Copyright © 1981 Educational Technology Publications, Inc., Englewood Cliffs, New Jersey 07632.

All rights reserved. No part of this book may be reproduced or transmitted, in any form or by any means, electronic or mechanical, including photocopying, recording, or by any information storage and retrieval system, without permission in writing from the Publisher.

Printed in the United States of America.

Library of Congress Catalog Card Number:
80-21332

International Standard Book Number:
0-87778-163-X

First Printing: January, 1981.

2144065

Table of Contents

DISPLAY BOARDS

1.

Introduction

Displays of various types are encountered everywhere in our environment. Many of these lie outside the traditional display realm, which relies heavily upon special surfaces, materials, and techniques to achieve certain predetermined goals. Nevertheless, there exists a definite relationship between the bulletin board display in the classroom and the rather less sophisticated display of produce in the grocery store. Both say, "Look me over and see what I have to sell—maybe you will want to buy something."

An attractive, well-designed bulletin board display is more likely to "sell" its message than one that lacks these qualities. A well-arranged, colorful display of fruits and vegetables will attract more buyers than will a haphazard one. In this book, the stress will be on "selling" information, not apples; however, the analogy is a good one and might be worth keeping in mind when creating and utilizing educational displays.

Among the display devices that will be stressed in this book are bulletin boards, chalkboards, pegboards, feltboards, magnetic boards, and hook-and-loop boards. Each of these serves a similar function, yet each is unique in its own special way. All, however, involve a more or less flat surface upon which the message, or portions of it, is displayed. The emphasis, then, will be primarily on two-dimensional materials, with three-dimensional materials being mentioned where it seems appropriate.

Additionally, such considerations as materials involved, composition, and sources will be covered, together with the principal theme of utilization.

Mention will be made of ways in which the materials can be utilized in both individualized and group instruction. Actual examples of the utilization of display materials will be given, and several student project activities will be suggested.

2.

Description of Display Boards

Display boards are typically large in their dimensions. They are structured in such a way as to accommodate a variety of materials upon their surfaces. The materials used in the display normally are related in one way or another, and, when taken together, communicate information and ideas about a certain subject.

Many different varieties of materials are often incorporated into a display. These might include such things as realia (actual objects), pictures, photographs, drawings, lettering, and three-dimensional models. Because of the diversity of such items, they often do not coalesce into a unified whole unless a special effort is expended to cause this to occur. The application of compositional principles in the arrangement of a display helps to unify it and to make it appear as one message rather than as a collection of separate ones.

Displays can be teacher-created, or, better still, student-created. The act of putting together a bulletin board display can be a valuable learning experience as well as an exciting social event.

Bulletin boards are among the most common varieties of display devices. They generally are of cork (often fabric-covered), composition board, or fiber material; pins and tacks can be pushed into their surface as a means of securing various items.

Chalkboards are also commonly found in most classrooms and are widely used. The old term "blackboard" is now *passe,* because very few surfaces are actually black these days. At one time, chalkboards were made of natural slate; however, modern boards are constructed of hardboard or steel. Some finishes are baked to the surface and are long-lasting and very serviceable.

Pegboards are made of Masonite and have holes over their entire surface. Different kinds of hardware can be used to secure objects to the surface. This type of board is useful when heavy materials are to be displayed.

Some room dividers are constructed of pegboard. These can be equipped with pegboard hooks and used for display purposes.

Feltboards may be purchased from suppliers but more often are homemade. Different kinds of fabric and other materials will adhere to the rough covering. Feltboards can be very colorful and contrasty, thus making them especially attractive to young children.

Magnetic boards are often chalkboards as well. Objects that have small magnets attached to them are readily attracted to the sheet metal face. Other materials, such as a steel screen, can also be used for the surface.

Hook-and-loop boards are covered with a fabric that has a weave composed of thousands of miniature loops. The item to be displayed has attached to it a section of fabric which consists of numerous stiff hooks. Upon pressing the hook material against the loop surface, the hooks engage the loops—the bond is amazingly strong and objects such as models and various kinds of realia can be readily attached to the board.

3.

Objectives

Although this book is not programmed and is not structured around behavioral objectives, it seems advisable and worthwhile to identify a number of competencies that can be attained through its use. It is difficult to specify such competencies in a manner that is all-inclusive, for it is hoped that information gleaned from this publication will serve to initiate further research into other ways that display materials can be developed and utilized. Therefore, the following list must be considered as a somewhat provisional one, subject to modification on the basis of the reader's needs, interests, and motivation.

After having read this book, you should be able to:

1. Define the terms "display materials" and "display boards."
2. Give a rationale for the use of display materials.
3. Describe six types of display boards or surfaces.
4. Describe ways in which visual materials can be created for use on each one of the six boards listed in No. 3 above.
5. List several different characteristics common to each of the six types of boards listed in No. 3 above.
6. List several ways in which you might utilize display boards in the classroom or similar environment; or, better, still, actually *use* them.

7. Describe how you might store and care for different types of display boards and their attendant materials.
8. Describe several precautions to take in order to insure that a presentation utilizing display materials will go smoothly.
9. Describe some ways in which you might arrange or compose a display; or, apply compositional ideas to the construction of a bulletin board dummy or to the construction of an actual display.
10. In general terms, tell how feltboards, magnetic boards, and hook-and-loop boards are constructed.
11. List several steps in caring for a chalkboard.
12. Describe two or three devices that can aid you in drawing or writing on the chalkboard.
13. Describe in detail several projects in which students might be involved.
14. Actually involve the students in such projects.
15. Locate terms in the Glossary; locate sources for equipment; locate sources for materials.

4.

Characteristics of Display Materials

Display boards of various kinds are available in virtually any and all classrooms. Utilizing a display board requires no special equipment, and no power cords, outlets, or provisions for darkening the room. A considerable number of varying visuals and verbals can be organized and displayed as a unit on a display board; such an arrangement provides the potential for a student to interact with the materials as often as desired and at his or her own rate. In this respect, the display becomes a sort of self-instructional, individualized lesson of a very basic kind.

Involving students in the development of objectives to be covered in the display, as well as in the creation and collection of materials and the design of the composition itself, can be meaningful and exciting for them. The act of putting together the materials on a large surface is one that involves teamwork as well as physical activity, both of which are important in the development of youngsters.

The bulletin board display can be put together inexpensively (often without spending a cent) from available pictures, clippings, handmade letters, etc. Chalkboards are always available to be used at a moment's notice when that certain idea pops into mind. Pegboards hold objects of considerable weight, while the hook-and-loop boards do the same thing with a little more "class." Feltboards are colorful and contrasty; many types of materials will cling to their surface, to be moved about as the need arises.

The characteristics mentioned above are, for the most part, positive in nature. Are there any disadvantages to the various kinds of display materials? Unfortunately, there are. Among such disadvantages is the fact that it takes a considerable amount of time to do a display (particularly true with the bulletin board). Even though many of the items to be displayed have been prefabricated, the act of assembling all of these on such a large surface is time-consuming. Also, the act of handling and pinning materials has a tendency to cause them to become tattered and worn with time.

The hook-and-loop board is very expensive, even in small sizes. Although such a board would be a useful item in a classroom, the cost often makes it impractical.

A rather vexing problem inherent in the feltboard is that of materials falling off the board at the most inconvenient times. Also, it can be difficult to achieve detailed effects on the felt patterns which are used on its surface.

Displays are of such a nature that it is difficult, in most cases, to cause them to be seen one minute, then out of sight the next (as with projected materials and picture sets). Therefore, the large, obvious display becomes, at times, a rather obtrusive element in the classroom; students continue to attend to it even after it has served its immediate purpose and other things are being considered.

5.

The Utilization of Displays

Bulletin Boards

Bulletin boards, as installed in the classroom, are securely positioned either on a wall or movable framework of some kind. They are compatible in color with the surroundings, sturdy, and of such a nature that pins and tacks can be pushed easily into the surface. Bulletin boards of a supplementary nature might be anything from a piece of heavy cardboard to a piece of cork. Regardless of the nature of the surface, all bulletin boards are meant to serve as the basis for an assemblage of related materials that form a larger whole. This characteristic gives a versatility to the display board that few, if any, types of classroom media can provide.

The bulletin board, because of its size, is a "natural" for the presentation of information to large groups. One problem with the large-group approach is that often verbal captions are too small to be seen by anyone who is not situated close to the board. One way in which this problem can be overcome, at least in part, is to "talk through" the display with the students as a group, clarifying whatever questions might arise at this time. Since the display will remain in position for a period of time, students have the opportunity to interact with it as interest and need cause them to do so.

A good strategy to employ when using the bulletin board is to leave it bare for periods of time—this is much like an

Figure 1

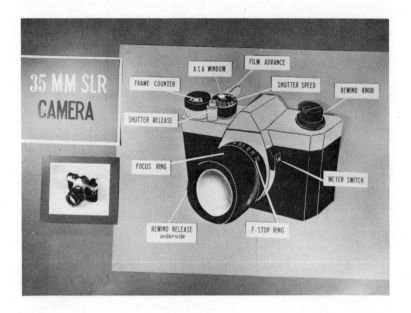

A Bulletin Board Display

intermission at a movie or stage play. The second act always seems a bit more exciting after a break. The display that is subsequently placed on the board represents such a marked change of pace from the bare surface that students automatically attend to it. One of the poorest ways in which to utilize the board is to leave the same display in position week after week. Such a display becomes so commonplace that no one pays any attention to it. An interesting experiment is to ask the students to write a detailed description of the school building or to create a drawing of it. Everyone will be quite surprised to find that many of the most important features are overlooked or distorted. This occurs because the surroundings are so familiar to the students that they tend to take them for granted—just as they come to take that old display for granted. Of course, upon entering the school for the first time (and for a certain period after that), the students explored their surroundings in depth and became well acquainted with them. However, after making the necessary adaptations to the environment, they turned their attention to newer and more interesting kinds of things. After a period of time, much of what initially seemed interesting was forgotten—just as with the bulletin board. So, the idea is that displays are effective only up to a point, at which time they should be dismantled and put aside in favor of other materials.

Displays are often used as stimuli that serve to create interest and excitement for a particular unit of work. They may not, in and of themselves, impart any great store of knowledge. However, they serve to cause the student to seek out knowledge from other sources. An example of such a display that was used successfully in a junior high school crafts class was a bulletin board made up of large trout fly patterns surrounding a brightly-colored caption which read, "Tie Your Own Flies." No instructions were given that would assist the students to tie their own flies, and no effort was made to identify the parts of the flies that were exhibited. However, the display led to many questions, and an extensive discussion subsequently led to the actual production of trout flies by the students.

A second type of display was used by the same crafts instructor to teach the students the steps involved in the production of the various types of flies. These media were in the nature of charts, rather than bulletin boards, and involved numbered, sequential diagrams of the tying processes. However, the charts were displayed on the bulletin board, three at a time, along with a large caption that read, "Fly Patterns for

Today"; and so, in a sense, the bulletin board was still the principal medium of communication. This type of application for the bulletin board might be called "formative," because it involves the developmental aspects of the lesson.

Finally, a display of the finished student-produced flies represents a use of the bulletin board that might be described as "summative," because it represents the end-result of everything that has happened before.

Needless to say, the students should be involved in the arrangement and design of the display whenever possible. The act of planning and constructing the display is a learning and socializing experience in itself, aside from the content considerations that will become paramount at a later time.

Bulletin boards that are utilized in a strictly individualized sense are rather uncommon, but, where used, are quite effective. Generally, the individualized course outline includes a section that is entitled, "Learning Options," or the equivalent. In this section are included all of the different materials that are available to the learner for his or her selection and utilization. The rationale for this is that various students learn optimally in different modes. For example, one individual might have a preference for purely audio types of experiences, while another might prefer purely visual (pictorial) types. This example is a bit far-fetched; in actual practice, most individuals prefer a mix (and, indeed, it may be impossible in most situations to present the concept in one pure mode or the other), but they like *different kinds* of mixes. So, the bulletin board, for example, provides an option which is different in many respects from a filmstrip. The bulletin board display is included in the section on learning options as one of the available options. It is listed along with the more traditional programmed books, slide sets, and audiotapes. The students are directed to interact with the display and are given supplementary information to assist them in working through the sequence. In actual

Figure 2

A Portable Folding Bulletin Board

practice, students would proceed through the program at their own pace until they reached the section on "Learning Options." Then, those who elected to work with the bulletin board display would acquire from the lab assistant or instructor any attendant materials required.

At this point, the students would locate the particular display with which they planned to work and would proceed through the learning sequence. As the individuals mastered the material, they would demonstrate competence in it. The advantages of such an approach are: (1) no hardware to malfunction; (2) several individuals can work through the display at any given time; (3) the display is generally inexpensive to put together; (4) if several students are interacting with the display, they can assist one another with any problems; and (5) the display can be left in position for any length of time and is, therefore, continuously available.

If the objective is to use the bulletin board for large-group instruction exclusively, then certain considerations must be addressed. Specifically, such a display must be simpler in nature than the individualized variety. Fewer visuals should be employed, and these should be large and clear. Titles should be large and concise; captions simple and of a large letter size. Lettering styles should be simple; sans-serif varieties are preferred. Clippings, such as those from newspapers, normally should not be used; these should be duplicated using a duplicating machine and should be distributed to the members of the class as supplemental handouts to be used in conjunction with the bulletin board display. In actual practice, however, few displays are meant to be used exclusively for immobile, large groups. Ideally, the members of the group should have open access to the display in order that they might interact with it in a number of ways.

Chalkboards

The chalkboard is the most common communication medium to be found in the classroom. It is virtually synonymous with the entire concept of a classroom, and few people could mentally picture a classroom that did not contain a chalkboard, or many chalkboards. They are so readily available that all too frequently their potential for varied approaches to the communication of information is overlooked, and they are used in one or two traditional (and often unexciting) ways. Although the wall-mounted, large-format chalkboard is the one which generally comes to mind when this type of medium is mentioned, several other varieties are available. For example, some maps and globes have chalkboard surfaces that are used with both white and colored chalks in much the same way as the traditional board would be used.

Folding chalkboard presentation easels are available that facilitate moving them from one area to another. These are compact and light-weight—features that make them popular with businessmen, salespersons, and lecturers, as well as with teachers.

A useful and interesting innovation is the paper chalkboard. This is made of specially-coated paper that is sturdy, erasable, and reusable. Small boards of such material are made by adhering the paper to a pasteboard backing; the boards are of such a size that they may be used by individuals at their desks. Paper chalkboards are available with various patterns, such as music lines, maps, cursive writing lines, printing lines, and graphs, printed in permanent inks on their surface. These can be marked and written on, erased, and used again by the individual working with the chalkboard.

Modern chalkboards are finished in colors that are harmonious with the decor of the room. Frequently, they are found in soft shades of gray, green, and even red—a far cry from the traditional black finish of yesterday. Such surfaces are easily cleaned, and, when high-grade chalks are used, they are relatively dust-free. Chalks in a wide range of colors are available that have been produced specifically for use on a chalkboard surface. Art chalks and pastels that are designed for use on paper should never be used on the chalkboard, because they cannot be erased. A wide variety of special tools for the chalkboard is described in another chapter of this book.

This medium lends itself to individual usage and can be adapted to small-group activities as well. Its direct use by large groups is rather restricted; however, indirect strategies can involve a total class group in its concurrent utilization. The basic limitation to the varied use of the chalkboard is the

Figure 3

Special Chalks in Holders for Use on Chalkboard

lack of imagination of the user; the creative individual will develop a limitless number of strategies for utilizing this common medium.

Individualized uses include the traditional technique of solving problems on the surface of the board. Typically, these are problems in math, but they need not be restricted to only this subject. One teacher made it a practice to place sentences on the board that included many mistakes in punctuation, spelling, sentence structure, etc. Individuals who wished to do so, or who needed some practice on such problems as spelling, were urged to go to the board and to make the necessary changes in the sentences until they were correct. This strategy was also useful for team kinds of activities (see below). Another individual, this time an art teacher, used an interesting technique for demonstrating the concept of perspective. She collected a number of large pictures that exhibited obvious linear perspective effects. Many of these were of structures, such as buildings and houses, but some showed roads, railroad tracks, and fences. Across each of the pictures, she ruled a horizon line—the basic beginning point for an illustration involving perspective. Students were encouraged to learn the principles of one-point and multiple-point perspective by placing these pictures on an opaque projector and projecting the image onto the chalkboard surface. By using a yardstick, they were then able to locate such essential structural elements as the vanishing point(s) and the lines of projection. These were drawn directly onto the board with chalk in such a way as to define the principal outlines of the structures in the projected pictures. When the projector was subsequently turned off, the board displayed the perspective skeleton of the picture. It became easy to analyze the basic rules of perspective from these diagrams.

Small-group instructional strategies are ideal for the chalkboard approach. Let us examine a few examples. It was suggested in the paragraph above that sentences of varying degrees of imperfection might be placed on the board for subsequent alteration by the students. This technique readily lends itself to small-group or team applications that can become a game or a contest. For example, two sentences of equal difficulty are placed on the board. Teams are selected, or are randomly chosen, and, at the word "go," each member of the team goes to the board, in turn, and makes one correction. If a student cannot effect a correction in a given length of time, a point is lost. The team that spots and corrects all mistakes first is the winner. Admittedly, this puts a bit of pressure on students who do not perform well in this area, so provisions might be made to handle this problem, such as allowing a short discussion time prior to the beginning of the game. During this period, mistakes could be spotted and different individuals assigned to make the predetermined corrections. This type of interaction can be helpful to those who need help with grammar. Also, this latter approach makes the effort more of a team effort and places the onus on the team rather than on a single individual.

An interesting small-group approach to chalkboard utilization that involves a kind of social interaction design utilizes the slide projector and homemade slides. Cartoons are cut from the newspaper, and the lettering in the balloons is covered with a piece of white paper. These cartoons are then photographed onto slides with a 35mm camera; the slides are then placed in the projector and projected, in a darkened room, onto the chalkboard. Many people assume that such projected images are not visible on the dark surface of the board. But this is not the case; the images are really quite brilliant. The effect of the image on the board is one of a cartoon with an accompanying empty word balloon. The idea of this exercise in creative verbal fluency is to initiate a story, which is continued frame-by-frame until some culminating statement can be made. The first frame is projected onto the board, and a student is selected to write a statement within the balloon that seems to be related to whatever the character in the slide is doing. The second slide is then projected, and a second student creates a statement for the next balloon, and so on, through the series. The captions might be read from the board and recorded on a cassette for a subsequent play-through of all of the slides. The act of working spontaneously on such a large surface, with its attendant, colorful, king-sized cartoons, can be a stimulating change of pace for students who are tired of the traditional paper-and-pencil approach to creative writing.

Another activity that involves small groups is the creation of a chalkboard mural. An activity such as this one is particularly pertinent when special occasions, such as Christmas, are being considered. The mural committee researches the subject, finds appropriate reference materials, makes sketches, then moves to the board to create the full-scale layout. Special chalks are used to finish the mural in full color; appropriate lettering styles are incorporated into the design. The finished mural is left in place for all to enjoy until the particular event has passed. Then, it is a simple matter to erase the board and make it ready for subsequent uses.

Another way in which the chalkboard can be used with small groups (or, better still, with two students) is to provide one student with a picture of something that he or she will describe verbally to the other student(s). The other student(s) draw(s) a picture (or pictures) on the board as the verbal description unfolds. The picture is then shown to the artist(s) and an assessment is made as to the degree of correspondence between the original and the drawing(s) of it. If several students are involved at the board, it is interesting to see which of them most adequately replicates the original.

The chalkboard is used traditionally for large-group instruction, due to its large size and immediate accessibility. Unfortunately, its full potential for this purpose is seldom realized, and it is often misused and over-used. Some suggestions for teacher-centered chalkboard utilization are:

1. Where possible, involve some pre-planning. Although one of the advantages of this medium is that it can be used to illustrate spur-of-the-moment ideas, it should not be used solely for this purpose.
2. Keep the board clean. Although the custodial staff may not condone such a practice, the use of a damp rag or sponge to remove excess chalk deposits from the surface is standard procedure and will not harm the board.

3. Never use chalks on your board that are designed for use on paper or cards. Utilize the special chalks that are manufactured specifically for chalkboards, but use these sparingly and for legitimate reasons rather than as fancy frills.

4. Use a variety of the special tools that can be purchased, or locally produced, for use on the board. Such things as large compasses, pounce patterns, and templates will make your illustrations more professional-looking as well as simpler to create.

5. Make certain that any lettering or writing that you place on the board is large enough to be seen by everyone who will view the display. A standard size for letters is about three inches, but this might vary according to viewing distance.

6. Materials on the chalkboard that you do not wish to be seen by the students can be covered by pulling a blind over them; or, you might simply cover such material with sheets of paper that are taped or tacked to the railing along the top of the board.

7. Information should be placed on the board prior to the class period during which it will be used. This principle applies when large amounts of material are involved. Of course, for short items and spontaneous ones, this is not a consideration. Avoid, whenever possible, spending class time to place a lengthy outline on the board—that is, unless the members of the class are involved in activities that release you to do such a thing.

8. Make your chalkboard work as attractive in appearance as possible. A bit of practice with lettering, writing, stick figures, etc., will permit you to be more proficient when the time comes to use this medium.

Figure 4

Chalkboard Templates

9. Use the medium as part of an overall "mix" of many kinds of media. Do not fall into the trap of using it to the exclusion of everything else; use it only when it seems to be the *best* available medium for a specific purpose.
10. Above all, don't place material on the board and then stand in front of it, thus making it impossible for students to see what is there.

Pegboards

Pegboards are normally created locally from sheets of

pegboard material that is available from a lumber yard. This material comes in standard 4 ft. x 8 ft. sheets that can be readily cut to any desired size with almost any kind of sharp saw. Two weights are available in this material; the heavier weight being the most satisfactory for larger boards. A frame of some kind is generally attached around the edge of the board to strengthen it, since the material is quite flexible, particularly in the lighter weight. The perforations in the board are located at one-inch intervals over its entire surface and extend completely through the board. This arrangement makes it possible to hang all types of materials from hooks that are placed in the holes. A variety of shaped supports is available for use with the pegboard, or, you may wish to create your own supports. Golf tees can be pushed into the holes and used as supports; aluminum clothesline wire can be cut into various lengths and bent into different shapes as needed.

Pegboards support a tremendous amount of weight, and, because of this, can be useful where realia and three-dimensional types of media are being displayed.

Many people paint the surface of the board (which is brown) with some attractive color of paint. It is quite expensive to use spray paint for this purpose; however, a roller loaded with latex or acrylic paint does a fast, inexpensive job that will be very serviceable.

The uses of the pegboard are more limited than are those for the bulletin board and the chalkboard. The pegboard is used primarily for large-group and small-group instruction in which the display of materials is central. However, a unique individualized application is described in the chapter entitled "A Case Study," which is included in this book.

Feltboards

Feltboards, or flannel boards, as they are often called, are most commonly found in the lower grades and in situations in which young children are involved.

Figure 5

A Pegboard

Feltboards consist of some type of sturdy support material (such as plywood) over which a sheet of felt or flannel has been secured. At times, the felt might be glued or tacked directly to a wall surface; at other times, it might be adhered to a portable surface. Feltboard figures of various kinds are purchased or manufactured to adhere to the felt. These are utilized in various ways in the communication of information to groups or individuals.

Some of the advantages for such a device include its colorful, contrasty nature. There is no display medium that can rival the feltboard for visual impact on the viewers. Felt

Figure 6

A Professor Clarifies a Complicated Idea
with the Feltboard

is a material that exhibits a saturated color surface of considerable intensity. By using various colors in combination, striking effects are possible that serve to attract attention. Another advantage is that this type of medium is inexpensive to make or to purchase and is simple in construction. The figures that are used on the surface are also inexpensive and easily produced. Additionally, feltboards are flexible—they can be used in any number of ways and with either individuals or groups.

Sequential kinds of concepts are readily illustrated with the feltboard because of the ease with which the various

Figure 7

*A Feltboard-Pegboard Combination for Use in
the Teaching of Arithmetic Concepts*

items can be removed and added to the surface. For example, a teacher of German found that prefixes and endings could be added easily to the roots of certain German words; this approach enabled him to create a set of such materials that could be used over and over, thus making the presentation exciting and colorful while saving time and effort.

When preparing to use the feltboard, you should conduct a preliminary run through the presentation in order to be certain that all elements to be utilized are present. It can be an embarrassing experience to find that some of the critical numbers or words are missing, just when you have reached

Figure 8

A Feltboard Designed by a Music Teacher

the point where you need them. Be certain also that some means for supporting the board is provided. This might be nothing more than a chalk tray in which the board can be positioned. Or, an easel might be available for this purpose. At times, a chair can be positioned on the table and the board placed against it, or a box can be used. You should also place some sample figures on the surface of the board that are then viewed from the maximum viewing distance in the room. These items should be visible to you from that position. If they are not, reposition the figures; otherwise your audience will not be able to follow the presentation adequately. A way in which to cope with this problem is to cluster the audience around you so that the maximum viewing distance is reduced.

When using this medium in an individualized mode, it is helpful to have several boards available. These need not be large in size, because they will be used in an intimate fashion. Smaller figures can be created for use with smaller boards; the converse is also true. Feltboards can be used in the development of many concepts, such as those of color families, fractions, shapes, etc. They are useful in the teaching of spelling, relationships, etc. They can be used to act out a story or to demonstrate cause-effect principles. Directions can be placed on a tape or can be given directly by the teacher. Older children might read the directions from a guidebook or from a simple handout. Games of various types might be devised that challenge the imagination of the individual. One such game involves the building of a person from a number of basic patterns that resemble heads, legs, etc. The idea is to create a particular kind of person, such as a police officer, doctor, fireman, or other person, and then to tell a story about what he or she would do in that particular job.

Small groups find it interesting to work through problems together. A larger board is useful for this purpose, because it gives more individuals access to its surface. Sequential kinds of problems are appropriate for solution on the feltboard.

Color relationships are illustrated through the manipulation of shapes that illustrate the primary and secondary segments of the color diagram. These are arranged in the proper order to show color families, color schemes, and value relationships. Graph lines that are permanently displayed on the feltboard surface permit the student to manipulate cut-out notes so as to diagram specific tunes, or merely to identify correctly the notes positioned differentially.

When using the feltboard with larger groups, the instructor

Figure 9

A Portable Flannel Board for Elementary Use

might illustrate a story that is being told by using appropriate figures. A flowchart might unfold step-by-step, or a PERT (Program Evaluation and Review Technique) system might be appropriate for use with older students. This medium might be used for mathematical drills or drills in spelling and grammar. Additionally, the quality of movable elements makes the feltboard useful for diagraming football plays, or for such things as illustrating hypothetical problems that students in the driver education class might encounter on the road. And, figures need not be made exclusively from felt. Pictures can be cut from magazines or can be drawn by the

Figure 10.

Pictures that are to be used on the feltboard can be drawn, or cut from magazines. These must be backed with a piece of felt or other rough material as shown.

students, and these can be backed with felt or some other suitable material to permit them to adhere to the surface of the board. Pellon, a material used for lining clothing, can also be used, as well as foam rubber in thin sheets, sandpaper, and many other kinds of material. If your figures always fall off the board, you may wish to apply a thin coat of pattern spray to the backside; this material is somewhat tacky and helps to keep the figure in place.

Magnetic Boards

Frequently, magnetic boards are combined with a chalk-

Figure 11

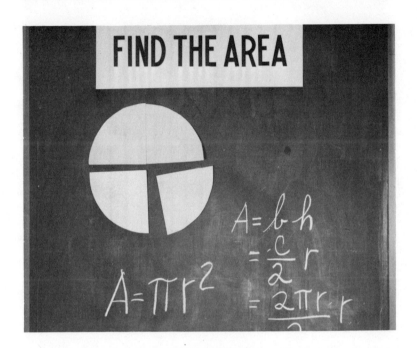

A Magnetic Board

board surface to give a specialized but useful type of medium. Because this board works the same way as the feltboard (items adhere to its surface), many of the suggestions for using the feltboard also apply to this medium. There are, however, some important differences between these two boards. The magnetic board uses as a base a sheet of steel painted or otherwise finished in some manner. The paint might be a chalkboard variety, in which case, the dual-purpose board mentioned above is the result. It is possible to have a magnetic flannel board, if this is desired, through the installation of iron screen under the felt surface. Small magnets (some of them of a rubber material that is impregnated with magnetic filings) are attached to whatever objects are to be displayed on the board. The magnets can be glued to the objects, or, they might have a gummed side and be self-adhering. Such objects can be readily displayed in any desired combination and pattern and can be easily moved without falling off the board. This approach is adaptable to almost any subject-matter area, but it seems to be most useful in the upper grades. The driver education teacher might wish to draw roads or intersections on the surface of the board. Hypothetical situations might be described and the students can be required to illustrate them through the placement of model cars. Or, the cars might be placed by the instructor and the students can be asked to identify certain law violations as illustrated by the models.

Again, the coach might find this medium useful to illustrate plays in football and basketball. To memorize the plays, students might be asked to make the appropriate moves using variously colored or marked "players." One teacher made a chess set that was magnetic. He created the chess figures from styrofoam, a light-weight material that is easily carved. To the base of each figure, he attached a magnet. This approach enabled him to work through a game or to show the standard movements of the various chessmen. Also, students could conduct a game in full view of their classmates, who could participate vicariously in the game, or even take turns in playing it. A geography teacher cut the various countries from a large map, thus creating a huge jigsaw puzzle from them. These were backed with magnets and were used in a game that involved placing the countries together in proper order in a given period of time.

Many other uses for this medium can be devised. The main constraints depend upon the degree of originality that an individual possesses.

Figure 12

Magnets are attached to the back of an object to make it suitable for use on the board.

Hook-and-Loop Boards

This medium is much like the feltboard with regard to utilization and construction. However, it supports objects much more tenaciously than does the feltboard. There are two basic fibers that are used with this type of medium. The base material is a fabric that has a surface which consists of a countless number of tiny loops. These are nylon and are extremely strong. The second type of material consists of adhesive-backed strips of fabric that have a surface covered with miniature hooks. The base material is attached to the object that will be exhibited on the board. When the two

Figure 13

A Close-up of Loop Material

fabric surfaces are pressed together, the hooks engage the loops with an amazing degree of tenacity. An arrangement such as this is capable of supporting objects of considerable weight without permitting them to slip in the least degree. One of the problems with this type of material is the cost; however, if your budget will permit such a purchase to be made, the hook-and-loop board can be an invaluable addition to the media in your institution.

An interesting application of this medium was in the "perting" by a university graduate school of the steps necessary in preparation for a visit from the accreditation

Figure 14

A Close-up of Hook Material

committee. The term PERT stands for Program Evaluation
and Review Technique. The approach involves establishing a
series of deadlines which are called "events"—these are
arranged sequentially with the times needed to reach the
events indicated. Such a procedure insures that an integrated
effort will be made possible and that those involved will
know precisely how the effort is progressing.

A hook-and-loop board was acquired; the events were
indicated on circles of cardboard that had the hook material
attached to their backs. The lines of the network were
indicated with narrow tape. This permitted a certain degree
of modification as needed.

Incidentally, the graduate school met its deadline and received the desired accreditation.

Other Types of Display Devices

Pocket racks can be purchased from commercial outlets, or they can be constructed easily from heavy craft paper or thin wood or Masonite sheets. Pocket racks have rows of shallow pockets across the front surface in which various flat materials can be placed. Letter cards can be arranged to spell words; word cards can be sequenced to create sentences; a picture series can be arranged in chronological order; poetry can be composed; root words can have suffixes and prefixes added; etc.

This device is particularly useful for individualized or small-group use, although it can also be employed in teacher-centered large-group strategies.

Erasable marker boards are hard-surfaced white boards upon which the presenter draws and writes with a special felt-tipped marker. The markers contain vividly-colored inks that, upon drying, can be erased completely and dustlessly with a cloth or chalkboard eraser. An advantage to this type of board is the brilliance and contrast produced by the marker on the white surface. Additionally, no residue is left on the board (as with the chalkboard) when the images are erased.

Also available are self-adhering erasable-color sheets that work just like the marker board described above. They have a surface that has a finish which is much like that of the board; i.e., white, slick, and hard. Where cost is a factor, the sheets can become a satisfactory substitute for the more expensive boards—they can be applied to chalkboards, bulletin boards, walls, or even to a piece of Masonite or cardboard. You can cut them to size with a pair of scissors; attaching is merely a matter of peeling away the protective backing sheet to expose the adhesive, and then applying the sticky surface to a base of some kind.

Figure 15

A Typical Pocket Chart

The erasable pens used with these sheets are the same as those used with the marker board, and they are erased in the same manner.

Changeable letter boards that can be wall-mounted or placed on stands make it easy to display verbal messages with a variety of plastic, wooden, and ceramic letters. Such boards have a fabric-covered fiber or cork surface into which pinned letters can be inserted. Other varieties have a grooved felt or plastic-covered surface. Special letters with rear extensions which match the grooves are used on boards of this type. The letters can be purchased in various sizes and colors; numbers and other characters are also available.

Figure 16

A Modification of the Pocket Chart

An interesting action device is the electric response board. Boards of this nature depend upon the completion of an electrical circuit for their reinforcement function to be effective. Typically, one portion of the board is devoted to words, labels, designations, etc., while a second portion deals with the pictorial equivalents to the words. For example, the names of a variety of animals might be listed on one half of the panel, while the pictures of the animals would be displayed on the other half. Terminals are located at each word and picture position. These are wired together in such a way that a student-initiated connection between the proper

Figure 17

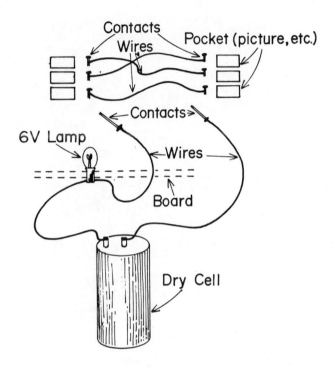

A Basic Diagram for Wiring of Electric Response

picture and its name completes the circuit and causes a light to blink or a bell to ring. If any combination but the proper one is made, no feedback is given.

The combinations can be continually changed and modified so that responses cannot be memorized. Also, the device can be adapted to handle material from almost any subject-matter area. It is necessary that a person have some basic knowledge of electricity in order to be able to construct such a device.

6.

The Care and Storage
of Display Boards

Certain types of boards are "self-storing" in the sense that they are permanently installed in the room. Such items as bulletin boards and chalkboards are often integral parts of the physical plant. Other types of display devices, however, are movable and, consequently, require storage.

Feltboards are generally light-weight, flat, and thin, at least in one dimension. They are, consequently, easily stored between sessions. The fact that they can be readily stored, however, becomes a problem of sorts, since some individuals tend to place them in any available corner where they become dusty and scuffed. It is a good idea to create some kind of envelope or cover for display boards that will be stored for any length of time. Heavy craft paper makes a suitable envelope; use tape, not staples, to hold it together. If you have no specially-prepared envelope in which to store boards, wrap them in an old sheet or slip them into a burlap bag. Figures such as those used on the feltboard should have their own storage envelope or box and should not be stuffed in a drawer—this is the surest way to lose critical parts.

Bulletin boards that are permanently installed on the wall also need a certain amount of care. The practice of placing pins and tacks in the surface will ultimately cause that surface to take on a texture that looks like the surface of the moon. This is easily remedied in several ways: Cover the board with burlap yardage. This material is available in a multitude of colors and sizes and is fairly reasonable in price. Or, use large pieces of colored butcher or construction paper as a cover; corrugated cardboard (it comes in colors and rolls) is also excellent. For a permanent repair job, paint the surface using a roller and a latex or acrylic paint in an attractive, subdued color. Two coats might be needed to cover the rough texture completely.

Chalkboards should be cleaned regularly with a suitable eraser. Large sponge and chamois-skin erasers are available and are preferable to the more common felt varieties. In spite of your constant effort to keep the surface clean, a chalk build-up will occur that ultimately will require a thorough washing with a clean rag or sponge and water. Wash a section at a time and dry it completely. If ghost images persist (generally caused by using chalk designed for paper, or inferior chalkboard chalk), you may have to scrub the board with a cleanser. Dampen your cloth and sprinkle a small amount of powder on to it. Clean just the smallest area possible (in an obscure corner). If any paint is removed by this process, stop immediately or you might damage the board beyond repair. Normally, good boards will be able to withstand such cleaning without becoming damaged.

After having cleaned the board, you must prime it by going over the surface with an eraser, which has been loaded with chalk dust. This renders the surface erasable and prevents the formation of most ghost marks that might otherwise occur.

Materials to be used on the various types of boards (such as pictures, photographs, drawings, etc.) can be mounted on cards using methods such as dry mounting or rubber cement mounting. Or, they might be covered with plastic or placed in plastic envelopes. These can be stored in file boxes, filing cabinets, envelopes, or portfolios. Three-dimensional materials are not so easily stored and require that spaces be set aside in cabinets or on shelves for their protection. Boxes might be utilized, but they take up considerable space in an otherwise crowded classroom. If an unused corner of the basement can be set aside for such storage usage, this can be an ideal place to store your materials until they are needed again. Be sure to put them in suitable containers or covers; basements are notorious places for dampness and dust.

7.

Environmental Preparation

One of the obvious first steps in preparing to utilize the various types of display materials is to make certain that sufficient display space is available. This is particularly pertinent where the bulletin board is concerned. In some buildings, particularly many older schools, few provisions have been made for bulletin board display. In instances of this nature, it may be necessary to resort to the use of movable boards of one kind or another. If excess chalkboard space has been provided (this occasionally happens), temporary panels can be placed over these surfaces to serve as display areas.

If, in spite of everything, you are unable to come up with sufficient display space, you may be forced to modify your approach so that it is compatible with what is available. This is the point at which idealism and realism clash head-on—and realism generally wins.

Another obvious consideration all too often overlooked is that of providing ample illumination for displays. Generally, normal lights in a room will serve this purpose, but there are times when additional light will enhance an effect. If you are unable to provide such light, you might want to consider the possibility of using lighter colors and values in your display. A light-colored background and brightly-colored cards and captions are often all that are needed to overcome the effects of a dark corner. Such considerations are not normally important in newer school buildings. Lighting engineers typically do an excellent job in distributing the light evenly and adequately over an area. However, many older buildings, and those that have been adapted to uses other than those intended, sometimes do suffer from a lack of adequate illumination.

Such supplemental items as easels of various kinds, stands, supports, hangers, and adjustable frames used with movable display boards must be provided, if they constitute essential factors in the use of the boards. At times, display boards might be leaned against a chair or a wall, but this is not always the best way to handle the problem. A bit of pre-planning will often make utilization more pleasant and effective.

If teacher-centered approaches are to be used, it is wise to arrange the seating in such a way that the display device is maximally visible to all individuals. This is not so important when individualized strategies are to be used, because students will have access to the media over a length of time rather than having but one opportunity to interact with them.

8.

A Case Study

All too often, students are required to memorize formulae without understanding the underlying bases for them. Some individuals find that such an approach often yields good results, but this is true only when the individual recognizes the appropriate instance for the application of a particular formula. Frequently, a rule seems to apply to a specific situation, when, in fact, it is totally inappropriate and produces an incorrect response. Nowhere in the curriculum does this occur more frequently than in the field of mathematics—both at the elementary level and also when more advanced concepts are being stressed.

Professors Stan Jencks and Donald Peck—both experts in the teaching of mathematics—recognized several years ago that a radically different approach to the teaching of math was needed in order that the problem mentioned above might become more of an exception rather than the rule. They determined that some means was needed whereby students would be enabled to build "visual imagery," or, in their words, "pictures in the child's mind." The tools which eventually evolved from their experimentation were, among others, the pegboard and the geoboard. The pegboard is constructed in two sizes, the larger one being 4 ft. x 4 ft., while the smaller one is 17" x 21" in size. Both are constructed of standard pegboard material with a reinforcing border of 1" square lumber attached around the edge of the backside of the board. The boards are coated with shellac and are then divided into squares, each of which consists of four rows of vertical holes and four rows of horizontal holes. Each square is outlined with a felt-tipped marking pen. The effect is one of ten vertical squares and ten horizontal on the large board, and four vertical and five horizontal (or vice versa) on the small board. Nails or golf tees are placed in the appropriate corner holes in order to describe a specific shape; then a rubber band or yarn is looped around the corner markers to enclose the shape. The larger boards are used for classroom demonstrations, while the smaller ones are used in small-group instruction.

The geoboard is designed to be used by the individual. Essentially, it is a modified pegboard, but there are some important alterations in the basic construction. A geoboard is only eight inches square; it has 16 squares drawn on its surface, each of which is a 1-1/2" square. Particle board in the 3/8" thickness is used as the basis for this device. Since this material has no holes, as does the pegboard, small nails are driven into the board at the intersection of every pair of lines. The final product, then, looks like a checkerboard of 16 squares with a nail placed at the corner of each square. This board is finished with shellac in the same fashion as the pegboard. Rubber bands are preferred because yarn is unmanageable on such a small surface.

Students could make their own geoboard through the use of a spirit duplicator handout which replicates the basic squared surface pattern. The handout is placed over the board, and the points at which the nails will be positioned are indicated with a hard pencil or ballpoint pen. The lines are then scribed on the surface, and the nails placed, etc., to complete the device.

Professors Jencks and Peck have devised countless strategies for using these display boards, but virtually all of them

Figure 18

A Geoboard

are based on the discovery method of learning. The learner is placed in a situation in which he or she is required to make his or her own decisions—a situation quite new and different to many students and teachers as well.

Through use of the geoboard and pegboard, both of which are physical objects that can be manipulated readily in endless ways, the threatening aspects of discovery learning are greatly reduced.

The pegboard is particularly useful when the concept of area is being stressed. The lesson proceeds in the following manner: the teacher has the children outline with yarn varying numbers of whole squares (referred to as "tiles"). This is simple for the children, and they soon exhaust all of the possibilities that exist. The next step is to release the yarn from one of the corners of a parallelogram to create a triangle; now, determining the area becomes more difficult, but, through a process of asking questions and eliciting feedback, the teacher soon has the students finding solutions to problems that become increasingly more complex. For example, the teacher says: "Make a triangle on your geoboards that looks like the one in the example on my pegboard." (This might be any kind of triangle, but initially it should be a simple right-angle triangle that is structured along the scribed lines on the board.) After all the children have duplicated the triangle, the teacher asks, "How many tiles does your triangle enclose?" After the children have agreed on the numbers that are enclosed, the teacher continues, "Talk quietly to your partner about as many ways as you can think of for making certain that your answer to this problem is correct."

After discussing the various methods that are described, the teacher moves to another right-angle triangle that is in a different position on the board, and the children are asked to solve the problem of area that is illustrated. The idea of "cutting and fitting" is discussed, and paper triangles that are drawn on graph paper are actually cut apart and the segments of tiles fitted together to reinforce the idea of fractional parts of an area. More complicated examples of the right-angle triangle are then covered, with continuous discussion until the concept is completely mastered. At this point, other types of triangles are considered, with the approach being similar to that used with the right-angle triangle. Finally, complex geometric shapes of all varieties are described on the pegboard, and concepts that have been learned in the triangle unit are generalized to these shapes.

The geoboard is an important adjunct to the pegboard in

the unit on area. Students work individually or in pairs with these devices and are able to create whatever shapes are described by the teacher. As the students progress, they invent their own shapes and invent ways in which to determine the area of the shapes that they have created.

Another application is in the multiplication of fractions—a concept with which many children have great difficulty. The teacher initiates the activity by saying: "Outline six tiles (for example) on your pegboard." Then, "Multiply your six tiles by two; how many tiles do you now have?" Eventually, after the concept of the multiplication of whole numbers is understood clearly, the teacher proceeds: "Now multiply your six tiles (for example) by two and a half." At this point, it is necessary for the children to move the pegs that have rested at the corners of the squares (the intersections of the lines) to a point that is halfway between a pair of lines, thus delineating one-half of a square. The teacher continues: "How many tiles do you now have?" It is necessary for the children to add the halves to obtain whole numbers to the extent that this is possible, and then to add this amount to the number of whole tiles to obtain the answer. From this simple beginning, it is easy to move to problems that include two mixed numbers. Before long, the children have mastered the concept of multiplying fractions and are able to generalize to everyday kinds of situations that call for this type of knowledge.

Numerous additional uses have been devised for the pegboard and geoboard by Professors Jencks and Peck as well as by creative teachers and students who have used these devices. The results of this approach have been extremely gratifying to those who have been involved directly and indirectly with the program. Initially, teachers work through the materials, using the same "discovery approach" that their students will use. In this way, they develop a sensitivity toward the student that is difficult to achieve in any other way. After they have mastered the basic concepts, the teachers then work with young people, either in contrived situations or in the actual classroom settings. Not only have professors, teachers, and students been excited and pleased by the results, but parents have also shown a large amount of enthusiasm for the approach. Students emerge from the program with an understanding of the logic of the various mathematical processes, rather than with a collection of memorized "rules." This understanding enables them to better analyze a problem and to logically arrive at the most appropriate way to deal with it.

9.

Future Trends
Related to Display Boards

It is difficult to predict any earth-shattering innovations in this area, mainly because most of what is being used today is basically about the same as it was a generation ago. Chalkboards have changed but not very much. Today, they are made of various materials, most of which are synthetic, whereas originally they were made of slabs of slate mined and finished through a rather laborious process. Feltboards have been around for years and so have bulletin boards. The pegboard is a more recent innovation, but it hasn't substantially altered the way that display materials are presented. The hook-and-loop board, one of the newest items, is limited in its application and so has caused no revolution. There is available today, however, a board that displays a unique surface unlike anything that has been produced thus far. These special boards are made of a plastic material that is a clean, white color. Instead of chalk, various kinds of marking pens and pencils are used on this surface, thus permitting the user to achieve brilliant, multi-colored effects on a surface that contrasts maximally. The white board is more visible than the darker chalkboard, and figures placed on it are more brightly colored and more contrasty. The end-effect of positive on negative (as opposed to the negative on positive of the chalkboard) appearances is very similar to the format of books and other materials with which students are familiar. This is not to say that the new board will ever supersede the old standby chalkboard, but it is at least a good supplement to it.

It is conceivable that other new surfaces will be invented that will be an improvement on the chalkboard and on the new multi-purpose boards described above. Such surfaces might be compatible with many more types of marking media and might have a treated surface that would permit various types of visual materials to be attached to it.

One exciting prospect for the future is the computer-controlled information display system. This system, which frequently takes the form of an electronics display board, is currently being used by stock brokers, NASA, the airlines, professional athletics, and so on. Until recently such display systems were too expensive to be widely applied in instructional settings such as public schools. But, with the advent of such technology as the memory chip and micro-computers, the complexity, size, and cost of such systems can now be reduced to the point at which they will become widely available in the future.

Through the use of such display systems, information stored in the computer memory bank in a digital code can be called up instantaneously. Additionally, on-line input is possible with some systems through the use of devices similar to the light pen or the beam pen. This means that, in effect, a teacher or student can "draw" directly on to the display with an electronic pen.

The format of systems of this type can be large in size for use in large-group instruction, or of a smaller size that is compatible with small-group or individualized teaching strategies.

10.

Using Common and Available Materials for Displays

Although you might be fortunate enough to have commercially-made display devices available to you most of the time, there will still be occasions in which you will have a need for something that is tailor-made. When such occasions arise, it is useful to know a few of the techniques that can be used to alter the materials that you have on hand or to start from scratch with the construction of totally new devices.

Attractive, sturdy feltboards can be purchased from a number of commercial outlets, but if the budget cannot support such purchases, you can make a usable board in several different ways. Many kinds of rough-textured cloth will work for this purpose, but flannel and felt are the perennial favorites. You might wish to staple the cloth to a section of pasteboard (furniture crates are good for this) or to a heavier type of material from a lumber yard. If you double the fabric, and then sew it together like a pillow-slip (one end open), you can simply slip this over the cardboard to make a serviceable unit.

Small, individual flannel boards are made by gluing fabric to the top of a cardboard box (such as a shoe box). The box itself then becomes the storage area for the various figures that will be used on the board.

Figures to be used on felt or flannel boards can be

Figure 19

Creating Drawing on Felt with Tube-Type Fabric Paint

purchased ready-made, or they can be created in the classroom. Various kinds of fabrics and papers are suitable for the figures, but materials that have a smooth surface (such as most papers) must have a rough-textured material glued to the back so that they will adhere to the feltboard surface. You can mark on fabrics with felt-tipped markers or liquid media of various kinds to create colorful, detailed figures.

Abrasive mesh can be glued to the backs of heavy items to make them adhere to the surface of the board. Other suggestions can be found in the various books that are available

Figure 20

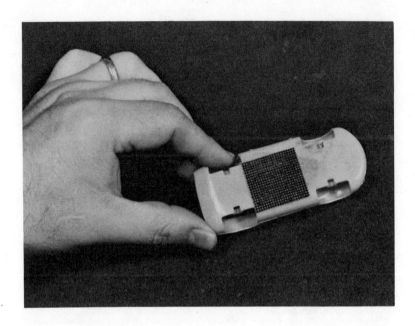

Abrasive mesh attached to the bottom of a plastic car; the car can now be attached to the feltboard.

on the subject of media production—refer to the chapter at the back of this text for references.

Because of the manner in which feltboards and magnetic boards are used, the consideration of composition is not an important one. This observation holds true to a lesser degree for the pegboard, hook-and-loop board, and, to a certain extent, the chalkboard. This leaves the bulletin board as the display device that demands the greatest consideration as far as composition is concerned.

A few general suggestions relative to arranging an attractive design on a bulletin board should be sufficient in order to begin in the right direction. With practice and study (neither of which need to be too painful), an individual can develop considerable competence in arranging artistic and informative displays.

First, let us consider the elements that are necessary in the construction of a bulletin board. As a rule, you will want to cover the board surface with something that is more attractive than the plain cork or composition material of which the board is constructed. This cover is referred to as the background; it is the base upon which the other items will be positioned. Backgrounds are important and should be selected with care. Textured materials, such as various kinds of fabrics and cardboards, make good backgrounds. Burlap in various colors works well, as does metal foil, construction paper, and even newspapers for special effects.

Along with the material itself, specific colors and values must also be considered. If most of the visuals to be displayed are light in value, then a dark background will be a good choice. If the visuals are brightly colored, a background of a more somber hue might be desirable.

The second element consists of the pictorial materials (the visuals). These should normally be mounted on cards of appropriate colors, carefully trimmed, and proportioned to present a neat appearance. A torn or tattered edge or an awkward proportion can detract from an otherwise good picture.

Finally, any captions, titles, or other lettered information constitute the third element. Such lettering should be well-rendered, neat, and bold. It should be large enough to be visible from the maximum viewing distance (in some instances, this might be a few feet, but in others, it could be the length of a room). Additionally, care should be taken in the selection of lettering style so that it will be compatible with the theme being followed.

Now let us consider color combinations. Try to match the

color with the theme of the display, just as you attempted to match the letter style with the theme. In other words, you might use a red, white, and blue combination if the idea is a patriotic one. A spring theme would employ pastel colors. A Halloween theme would look peculiar if it were rendered in yellow-greens, pinks, and sky blues. Think of the mood that you wish to convey; then select the combinations of colors that will project this mood and use these for backgrounds, mounting boards, illustrations, and lettering blanks.

A way in which to test various color combinations prior to constructing the actual bulletin board display is to create miniature "roughs" or "dummies" of the composition. These need not include actual lettering, or even actual pictures. Blanks of paper can serve for both of these. The composition as well as the color pattern should be incorporated into the dummy. When a suitable color-design combination is found, then the construction of the actual bulletin board design should be initiated.

One approach to composition (the arrangement of the various pictures, captions, headings, charts, etc.) is to position the various components over one of the basic letter forms. Letters such as C, H, L, O, S, and T are useful basic shapes around which to structure a design. Consider the "C," for example—staple colored paper to the background in the shape of a huge "C." Arrange the pictures over the colored paper, attach the various captions. Then, you may wish to position the main heading somewhere within the open area of the "C" to complete the design. Several illustrations of this approach have been included in this chapter.

Creating titles for bulletin boards can be a special problem. Titles should stand out from the rest of the display and should attract the viewer's attention maximally. These should be short and to the point and should include key words that inform at a glance. Use action words in the caption; placing the verb first is an effective way in which to construct a

Figure 21

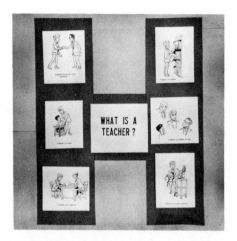

The basis for this bulletin board design is the letter 'H.'

Figure 22

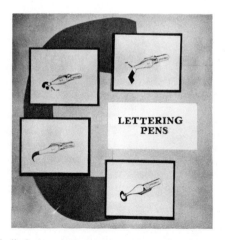

This bulletin board composition is based on the letter 'C.'

Figure 23

This bulletin board composition is based on the letter 'Z.'

compelling main caption. For example, you might use "Fight Pollution—Everyone's Enemy," in place of "Pollution Is Everyone's Enemy—Let's Fight It."

The caption is also effective if stated as a question. For example, "Ways in Which We Can Improve Our Environment" becomes "How Can We Improve Our Environment?"

When selecting letters for use in the display, you might wish to consider some of the many kinds of pre-made letters that are available. (See the list of suppliers included in this book.) Three-dimensional letters, cardboard varieties, cutouts with sticky backs, etc., are all effective. However, if you cannot afford to purchase such letters, or, if you would prefer to create them or to have your students do this, many different patterns are illustrated in books on lettering and production. Or, you may wish to design your own display alphabet—just make certain that the letters are clean and legible, particularly if young children are the audience.

You may wish to contact the media center in your school or district to see if it has any of the various lettering devices available for you to use. Such things as stencils, pens and guides, scribers, templates, and rubber stamps will make your lettering much simpler as well as more professional-looking.

Before you assemble the finished display, you may wish to prearrange it on the floor or on a table so that you can assess its overall appearance before securing it to the board. When you are satisfied that the display is ready to be mounted, select the proper mounting devices for this purpose.

It is not a good idea to use pins or thumbtacks to secure your materials to the bulletin board if you can help it. Such materials not only cause the corners of the visuals to become tattered, but they are unsightly in a display. Some of the more popular adhesives that are used for sticking materials to display surfaces are the Scotch mounting squares (pressure-sensitive squares that are pressed onto the back of the item to be hung), Dennison Glutaks (drops of dry, pressure-sensitive adhesive on release paper), Milton Bradley Adhezo-Tack (reusable, doesn't stain), Stikki-Wax adhesive sticks, and double-sided tape. Such materials are unobtrusive—even invisible—when compared with tacks. If you must use pins or tacks, place eyelets in the corners of the materials; at least then your pictures won't be torn. If you do not have access to double-sided tape, merely roll a short length of regular masking tape into a loop with the sticky side facing out. Then position this under each corner on the picture and press it against the surface of the board. Presto! Instant adherence with only the picture showing.

In some areas, schools are prohibited by law from hanging certain kinds of displays. The criterion seems to be whether or not the materials are deemed to be a fire hazard.

Flammable pictures, paper designs, and three-D kinds of objects that might be combustible are considered inappropriate for display unless they are contained within the confines of the board; and, even then, there may be some question if too much is concentrated in one space. Before placing anything on your board, check to see if such a law exists in your district. Even if it does not, it only makes sense to use discretion where the chance of fire is concerned.

Incidentally, bulletin board cut-outs of an endless variety of animals, people, etc., are manufactured by a number of firms, including Bemis-Jason, Dennison, Instructo, and Eureka. Check with your nearest school supply outlet for these materials.

Now that your bulletin board is assembled and ready for use, you should evaluate it. Ask yourself these questions:

    a. Does it attract attention?

    b. Is the main theme clearly illustrated?

    c. Is the layout simple and uncluttered?

    d. Is the color scheme appropriate?

    e. Is the lettering legible?

    f. Do the illustrations, lettering, and background all seem to belong together? In other words, is the design unified?

Let us consider chalkboards for a moment. Most of the chalkboards that are used for instructional purposes are of the commercial variety and are permanently mounted to a wall. If you should wish to construct a portable board, you can purchase a special "slate-surfaced" paper that can be glued to just about any flat surface with spray adhesive or dry mount tissue. Or, you can acquire a can of "liquid slating" which is sprayed or brushed onto a surface of some kind. At times, you might locate an old school that is being razed—this is an excellent opportunity for you to pick up a piece of old chalkboard that can be trimmed and cleaned, placed in a frame, and used as a portable unit.

When creating a magnetic chalkboard, you will want to use some kind of sturdy material such as Masonite as a base. Because the metal that will be used is quite heavy, it needs a strong base in order to support it and keep it rigid. Treat the metal with a solution such as vinegar in order to render the galvanized surface compatible with the paint. Use contact cement to attach the base and the metal together; coat both of the surfaces, let them dry, then press them together for a permanent bond. The paint can be applied with a brush or roller, or you might prefer to use spray paint for this purpose. Adhesive-backed sheets can also be purchased that are adhered to the surface; no painting is necessary. Magnets are available that are of a rubberized material. These can be cut to size with a pair of scissors, so it is a simple task to prepare objects for display on the board.

Many different devices are available for use in placing diagrams on the chalkboard. Among these are large compasses that have a rubber-tipped leg instead of the typical metal point, templates of various kinds (these can be easily made from plywood or Masonite), pounce patterns (cardboard drawings that have holes punched around the critical outlines—a chalkboard eraser is "pounded" over the holes to create a dot pattern on the board), and the opaque projector (used to project a diagram onto the board which is then outlined in chalk). Such devices make the utilization of the chalkboard much more simple and effective than it might otherwise be.

Pegboards are easily constructed from pre-made perforated Masonite panels that are available from the lumber yard. Wire clothes hangers can be cut and bent in various ways for use in supporting all kinds of flat and 3-D display materials.

Many specialized types of display devices can also be created from odds and ends. Two such displays are illustrated in this chapter. The sentence board is merely a section of plywood to which looseleaf rings have been secured. Words

Figure 24

Attaching Magnets to Back of Magnetic Board Figure

Figure 25

Using the Chalkboard Template

Figure 26

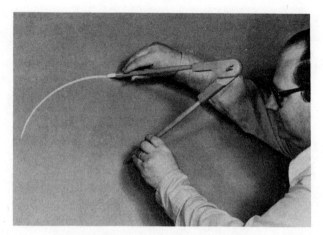

Using the Chalkboard Compass

Figure 27

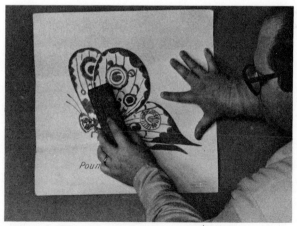

Creating Chalkboard Illustration with Pounce Pattern

Figure 28

A Sentence Board in Use

that correspond to the parts of speech are lettered on cards punched and fastened over the rings. Students can create all kinds of interesting (and sometimes zany) sentences with this board.

The second type of display consists of a mirror which represents the face of a girl who is constructed of colorful and frilly materials. This device was used by a teacher who was interested in developing the self-images of her young students. The girls, when looking at the display, saw their own faces looking back at them. Various activities and games were devised to make the sessions meaningful.

Many other kinds of special display materials can be created from inexpensive and available materials by the imaginative teacher. For additional ideas and explicit instruc-

Figure 29

The face on this display is a mirror. A child looking at the display sees her own face on the little ballerina.

tions on this subject, there are many good books and programs that are available and which can be an invaluable resource. A number of these have been included in chapters at the back of this text.

11.

Student Projects

1. *Create bulletin board dummies.* This is a class project. Students are encouraged to create a bulletin board rough or dummy from materials that are provided. All projects are submitted, and the "best" one is selected to be used as the basis for the actual display. A good way to handle the selection process is to have a local artist or display person come to the class, where he or she critiques the projects and makes the selection. Another approach is to form committees, each consisting of several students who work together to produce a dummy that has been designed by the group. Each dummy is used as the basis for a particular display throughout the year. Special days, such as Christmas, Thanksgiving, etc., are natural themes for displays. Subject-matter related themes, such as historical or artistic ones, can also be used. The committees are responsible for putting displays together based on the dummies.

2. *Make a chalkboard mural.* Another group activity—students create a small rough of the mural. This is placed in an opaque projector to be projected onto the board and traced. Special chalks are used to color the mural.

3. *Make an electric board.* Electric boards are special display boards based on the concept of positive reinforcement for correct responses. They are designed to be used by individual students and are so structured that a correct

response completes an electrical circuit, thus giving a signal of some kind. Students can construct such a board with simple materials and instructions—heavy cardboard will serve as the base, copper wire conducts the current, a regular dry-cell battery furnishes the power, and nails attached to a length of wire are the probes. One manner in which the boards are set up is to have pictures on one side of the board and words on the other; an equation on one side with the equivalent statements on the other. Analogies can be used; color mixtures work well; etc. To complete the circuit, the student touches the probes to the matching items on either side of the board; if a match is not made, the circuit is not completed and a signal is not produced.

4. *Create feltboard figures to illustrate a concept or a story.* The concept of "square" or "round," among others, is handled nicely with the feltboard. Older students might choose a concept and then develop the necessary figures to illustrate and to teach it to younger students or to students who are not familiar with the concept. Young students enjoy creating their own figures from paper or material for use in illustrating a story that they tell verbally.

5. *Create a feltboard mannequin.* This is a good project for young people who are interested in fashion design. A figure of a person is cut from some kind of board (cardboard, foam-core, etc.); felt is adhered to the board in the form of a basic dress. Various embellishments are then cut from different colors of felt or from other materials that will adhere to the felt. These are used to alter the basic dress. Through addition and subtraction of such embellishments, a standard dress pattern can take on all kinds of appearances.

6. *Make a skeleton.* This is a project for physiology, anatomy, health education, etc. If a hook-and-loop board is to be used, the parts of the skeleton are cut from four-ply poster blanks. The hook material is then adhered to the backs of the parts. If the feltboard is to be used, then white felt or

Pellon is good. The parts are put together in the same manner as a jigsaw puzzle would be assembled. An interesting game can be built around this exercise: The students draw cards from a deck or box. The names of the various bones are listed on the cards. The student continues to draw until he or she is unable to identify and position the bone listed on the card; another student then takes over and continues until he or she misses. The individual who gets the greatest number of points is declared the winner.

7. *Write your own song.* Using a chalkboard that has semi-permanent lines drawn on its surface (chalk soaked in sugar water will make lines that will not erase but that can be washed off with water), create your own music by drawing the notes in the desired position on the board. Try the tune on the piano or have the music teacher do this. If it needs some modifications, erase the notes and change them until you create a tune that you like.

8. *Make a montage.* A montage is created by combining different pictures, photos, and drawings into a single, unified pattern. This is a good group activity that can involve any number of students in the construction of a king-size layout on the bulletin board.

Bibliography

Audiovisual Instruction. Association for Educational Communications and Technology, 1201 16th Street, N.W., Washington, D.C. 20036 (Periodical).

Brown, James W., and Richard B. Lewis. *AV Instructional Materials Manual: A Self-Instructional Guide to AV Laboratory Experiences.* New York: McGraw-Hill Book Co., 1969.

Brown, Robert M. *Educational Media: A Competency-Based Approach.* Columbus, Ohio: Charles E. Merrill Publishing Co., 1973.

Bullough, Robert V. *Creating Instructional Materials.* Second Edition. Columbus, Ohio: Charles E. Merrill Publishing Co., 1978.

Calder, Clarence R., Jr., and Eleanor M. Antan. *Techniques and Activities to Stimulate Verbal Learning.* New York: Macmillan Company, 1970.

Dale, Edgar. *Audio-Visual Methods in Teaching.* New York: The Dryden Press, 1953.

Erickson, Carlton W.H., and David H. Curl. *Fundamentals of Teaching with Audiovisual Technology.* Second Edition. New York: McGraw-Hill, 1972.

Frye, R.A. *Graphic Tools for Teachers.* Mapleville, R.I.: Roadrunner Press, 1975.

Gerlach, Vernon S., and Donald P. Ely. *Teaching and Media: A Systematic Approach.* Englewood Cliffs, N.J.: Prentice-Hall, Inc., 1971.

Indiana University. *Improving the Learning Environment.* Washington, D.C.: U.S. Department of Health, Education, and Welfare, Office of Education, 1963.

Jencks, Stanley M. *Geoboard Investigations.* Salt Lake City: Gem Printing Co., 1968.

Jencks, Stanley M., and Donald M. Peck. *Building Mental Imagery in Mathematics.* New York: Holt, Rinehart, and Winston, Inc., 1968.

Kemp, Jerrold E. *Planning and Producing Audiovisual Materials.* Third Edition. New York: Thomas Y. Crowell, 1975.

Kinder, James S. *Using Instructional Media.* New York: D. Van Nostrand Co., 1973.

Koskey, Thomas. *Flannel Boards.* Palo Alto: Fearon Publishers, Inc., 1961.

Koskey, Thomas. *Baited Bulletin Boards.* Palo Alto: Fearon Publishers, Inc., 1966.

Kuppers, Harold. *Color: Origin, System, Uses.* New York: Van Nostrand Reinhold Co., 1973.

Laliberte, Norman, and Alex Mogelon. *Silhouettes, Shadows, and Cutouts.* New York: Reinhold Book Corp., 1968.

Learning. Education Today Company, Inc., 530 University Avenue, Palo Alto, California 94301 (Periodical).

Learning Resources. Association for Educational Communications and Technology, 1201 16th Street, N.W., Washington, D.C. 20036 (Periodical).

Linker, Jerry Mac. *Designing Instructional Visuals.* Austin: University of Texas, 1968.

Lockridge, J. Preston. *Better Bulletin Board Displays.* Austin: University of Texas, n.d.

Minor, Ed. *Simplified Techniques for Preparing Visual Instructional Materials.* New York: McGraw-Hill Book Company, 1962.

Minor, Ed., and Harvey R. Frye. *Techniques for Producing Visual Instructional Media.* New York: McGraw-Hill Book Company, 1970, 1977.

Morlan, John E. *Preparation of Inexpensive Teaching Materials.* San Francisco: Chandler Publishing Co., 1963.

Mundt, Ernest. *A Primer of Visual Art.* Minneapolis, Minn.: Burgess Publishing Co., 1950.

Popham, W. James. *Evaluating Instruction.* Englewood Cliffs: Prentice-Hall, Inc., 1973.

Randall, Reino W., and Edward C. Haines. *Bulletin Boards and Displays.* Worcester, Mass.: Davis Publishing Co., 1961.

Satterthwaite, Les. *Graphics: Skills, Media, and Materials.* Dubuque, Iowa: Kendall/Hunt Publishing Co., 1972.

Thomajan, P.K. *Handbook of Designs and Motifs.* New York: Tudor Publishing Co., 1950.

Thomas, R. Murray, and Sherwin G. Swartout. *Integrated Teaching Materials.* New York: David McKay Co., Inc., 1963.

Weseloh, Anne Douglas. *E Z Bulletin Boards.* Palo Alto: Fearon Publishers, Inc., 1959.

Williams, Catherine M. *Learning from Pictures.* Washington, D.C.: Department of Audiovisual Instruction, NEA, 1963.

Wittich, Walter A., and Charles F. Schuller. *Instructional Technology: Its Nature and Use.* Fifth Edition. New York: Harper and Row, Publishers, 1973.

Wittich, Walter A., Charles F. Schuller, David W. Hessler, and Jay C. Smith. *Student Production Guide to Accompany Instructional Technology.* Fifth Edition. New York: Harper and Row, Publishers, 1975.

Glossary

Achromatic colors. Colors that do not possess the characteristic of hue; that is, black, white, and gray.

Acrylic paint. A plastic-based paint which is soluble in water until it has hardened.

Bulletin board. A large display surface upon which various elements are organized as a message.

Bulletin board wax. A pliable adhesive that is used to adhere materials to the surface of the board.

Caption. The lettered or printed information that generally accompanies the visual materials in a display.

Cellotex. A fibrous building material that is manufactured in large sheets. It has a surface that is compatible with paints, tacks, pins, etc., that make it a good material from which to make display boards.

Chromatic colors. Colors that possess the characteristic of hue; that is, red, blue, green, etc.

Composition. The union of various elements to make a larger whole; involves the application of some kind of principles.

Contact cement. A rubber cement-like material, coatings of which have a great affinity for one another. Two surfaces are coated and permitted to dry; when pressed together, they adhere tenaciously.

Dry mount tissue. A heat-sensitive tissue that is impregnated with wax, which, upon melting, adheres to a surface. Highly permanent.

Dummy. A rough approximation of the finished product, generally on a small scale.

Electric board. A response board that is based on the idea of positive reinforcement. When a correct response is made, a circuit is completed and a light is turned on or a bell rings, etc.

Feltboard. A display board that has a textured surface to which similarly textured materials will adhere.

Ghost image. A faint remnant of a prior figure that is left on the chalkboard after erasures have been made. Generally the result of using an improper type of chalk.

Gothic letter. A plain-looking letter that has strokes of an even width throughout.

Hardware. Equipment, such as projectors, tape recorders, TV sets, etc., through which messages are relayed.

Hook-and-loop board. A board covered with a synthetic fiber that consists of numerous small loops is termed a "hook-and-loop board." The material that adheres to this surface is composed of a fabric whose surface consists of miniature hooks.

Lamination. A plastic material that is adhered to a picture or other surface as a protective covering.

Liquid slating. Chalkboard paint; can be applied with a brush or roller. Or, it can be purchased in a spray can. Used in the manufacture of chalkboards.

Magnetic board. A board with a magnetic surface to which objects backed with small magnets will adhere.

Masonite. A very hard, commercially-manufactured board that is used in the construction of furniture and other such items. Two kinds are available—tempered and untempered.

Montage. A collection of pictures, drawings, and other visual materials that are tightly composed into a unit by cutting them out and gluing them to a common background.

Opaque projector. A projector that uses reflected light to project the image of an opaque item onto a surface.

Pattern spray. A type of adhesive that is used to adhere a pattern to a section of fabric while the fabric is being cut to shape. Non-permanent; useful with feltboard figures.

Pegboard. A board made of Masonite with small holes over the entire surface. Useful for supporting heavy display materials.

Pellon. A light-weight material that is used by dressmakers. Useful for feltboard figures.

Rough. See "Dummy."

Rubber cement mount. A combination of picture and backing that have been coated with rubber cement and pressed together.

Sans-serif letter. See "Gothic letter."

Software. Generally the pictures, captions, printed and duplicated materials, etc., in which the message is contained. (See "Hardware.")

Spray adhesive. A material (generally a type of liquid wax) that is used to adhere materials together. It is sprayed on one or both surfaces for a mount that varies in permanence according to the manner in which the spray has been applied.

Tack board. A board that has a surface which is sufficiently soft to permit pins and tacks to be readily inserted into it.

Equipment Manufacturers
and Distributors

Acme Bulletin Board and Directory Company, 37 East 12th Street, New York, New York 10003 (display boards).

Advance Products Co., P.O. Box 2178, Wichita, Kansas 67201 (easels).

Beckley-Cardy Co., 1906 North Narragansett, Chicago, Illinois 60639 (feltboards, bulletin boards).

Charles Beseler Co., 219 South 18th Street, East Orange, New Jersey 07018 (opaque projectors).

Brunswick Corporation, 2605 East Kilgore, Kalamazoo, Michigan 49003 (chalkboards).

Corbett Blackboard Stencils, 548 Third Avenue, North Pelham, New York 10803 (chalkboard devices).

Dick Blick Company, P.O. Box 1267, Galesburg, Illinois 61401 (lettering equipment).

Educational Supply and Specialty Company, 2833 Gage Avenue, Huntington Park, California 90255 (display equipment).

General Binding Corporation, 1101 Skokie Blvd., Northbrook, Illinois 60062 (laminating equipment).

The Instructo Corporation, Paoli, Pennsylvania 19301 (feltboards).

Keuffel & Esser Co., 15 Park Row, New York, New York 10038 (lettering guides and scribers).

Koh-I-Noor, Inc., 100 North Street, Bloomsbury, New Jersey 08804 (lettering guides).

Letterguide Co., P.O. Box 4863, Lincoln, Nebraska 68509 (lettering guides and scribers).

Magna Magnetics, 777 Sunset Boulevard, Los Angeles, California 90046 (magnetic boards).

Seal, Inc., Roosevelt Drive and B Street, Darby, Connecticut 06418 (dry mounting presses).

Silver Burdett Company, 460 South Northwest Highway, Park Ridge, Illinois 60068 (display equipment).

Varigraph Company, 1480 Martin Street, Madison, Wisconsin 53701 (lettering guides and scribers).

Weber-Costello Co., 1900 Narragansett Avenue, Chicago, Illinois 60639 (magnetic boards).

Wood-Regan Instrument Co., Inc., 184 Franklin Avenue, Nutley, New Jersey 07110 (lettering templates and pens).

Materials Manufacturers and Distributors

Artype, Inc., 345 East Terra Cotta Avenue, Crystal Lake, Illinois 60014 (pressure-sensitive letters).

Beckley-Cardy Co., 1900 North Narragansett, Chicago, Illinois 60639 (3-D display and cut-out letters, bulletin board figures).

Brandywine Photo Chemical Co., Inc., P.O. Box 298, Avondale, Pennsylvania 19311 (spray adhesive).

Carter's Ink Company, Cambridge, Massachusetts 02142 (pens, ink).

Chart-Pak Rotex, 4 River Road, Leeds, Massachusetts 01053 (pressure-sensitive letters).

Dennison Manufacturing Co., Framingham, Massachusetts 01702 (cut-out letters).

Eastman Kodak Co., 343 State Street, Rochester, New York 14650 (dry mount tissue).

Edmund Scientific Co., Barrington, New Jersey 08007 (magnets).

The Highsmith Co., Inc., P.O. Box 25, Highway 106 East, Fort Atkinson, Wisconsin 53538 (all kinds of display boards, lettering, etc.).

W.W. Holes Mfg. Co., St. Cloud, Minnesota 56301 (cut-out letters).

Hunt Manufacturing Co., 1405 Locust Street, Philadelphia, Pennsylvania 19102 (pens, ink).

Instantype, Inc., 7005 Tujunga Avenue, North Hollywood, California 91605 (ready-made lettering).

Koh-I-Noor, Inc., 100 North Street, Bloomsbury, New Jersey 08804 (pens, inks).

Leah AV Service, 182 Audley Drive, Sun Prairie, Wisconsin 53590 (bulletin board adhesive).

Letraset, Inc., 2379 Charles Road, Mountain View, California 94040 (pressure-sensitive letters).

Quik—Stik Company, P.O. Box 3796, Baltimore, Maryland 21217 (vinyl plastic and cut-out cardboard letters).

Redikut Letter Company, 12617 South Pacific Avenue, Hawthorne, California 90250 (3-D letters).

Seal, Inc., Roosevelt Drive and B Street, Derby, Connecticut 06418 (dry mount tissue, lamination film).

Stik-A-Letter Company, Route 2, Box 1400, Escondido, California 92025 (cut-out lettering).

Stripprinter, Inc., P.O. Box 18-895, Oklahoma City, Oklahoma 73118 (photographic lettering supplies and equipment).

Annotated List of Media

BETTER BULLETIN BOARDS. 16mm motion picture, color or black and white, sound. Indiana University, 1956. Covers basic layout of the board; lettering, dynamic composition, and materials. Also suggests ways in which the student can be involved, or at least considered, in the construction of bulletin boards.

BULLETIN BOARDS AND DISPLAYS. 35mm filmstrip with script, color. Bailey-Film Associates, 1966. Covers good design and composition. Includes many colorful illustrations of different compositions. Covers various kinds of materials that can be used in construction.

BULLETIN BOARDS: AN EFFECTIVE TEACHING DE-VICE. 16mm motion picture, color, sound. Bailey-Film Associates, 1956. Shows a class involved in the planning and execution of bulletin boards. Shows 12 examples of class-prepared boards.

BULLETIN BOARDS FOR EFFECTIVE TEACHING. 16mm motion picture, color, sound. University of Iowa, 1953. Covers the process of creating a bulletin board from start to finish. Includes such things as the central topic, materials, color, composition, lettering, etc.

CHALK AND CHALKBOARDS. 16mm motion picture, color, sound. Bailey-Film Associates, 1959. Begins with the basics of chalkboard construction. Considers ways in which chalkboards can be utilized. Illustrates several characteristics of this device which make it unique. Goes into detail on the care of the board. Also illustrates a number of special devices (such as templates) that can be used.

CHALKBOARDS AND FLANNEL BOARDS. 35mm filmstrip with script, color. Bailey-Film Associates, 1967. This filmstrip covers the use, care, and construction of these display devices.

DESIGN WITH PAPER. 16mm motion picture, color, sound. International Film Bureau, 1961. Starts with simple basic folds and moves to more complex forms. Useful where 3-D display materials are desired.

DISPLAY AND PRESENTATION BOARDS. 16mm motion picture, color, sound. International Film Bureau, 1971. Covers the nature, construction, and utilization of felt, hook-and-loop, magnetic, electric, peg, and other types of display boards.

EXCITING BULLETIN BOARDS. 35mm filmstrip, color, sound. McGraw-Hill, 1963. Covers the ways in which a diverse collection of materials can be combined to form effective bulletin boards.

THE FELTBOARD IN TEACHING. 16mm motion picture, color, sound. Wayne State University, Michigan, 1951. Describes ways in which this device might be used in the classroom.

FLANNEL BOARDS AND HOW TO USE THEM. 16mm motion picture, color, sound. Bailey-Film Associates, 1958. Covers the construction and utilization of the flannel board. Suggests ways in which materials for use on felt and flannel surfaces might be created.

HOW TO KEEP YOUR BULLETIN BOARD ALIVE. 35mm filmstrip, color. Ohio State University, 1951. Emphasizes the problems that seem to be inherent in many bulletin boards; suggests ways to correct them.

THE MAGIC OF THE FLANNEL BOARD. 16mm motion picture, color, sound. Instructo Products, 1964. Shows the use of various kinds of flannel board cut-outs in the teaching of math and reading. Uses a creative approach which is designed to stimulate students and cause them to want to learn.

Appendix A

Sources of Free and Inexpensive Materials for Use in Displays

Associations and Councils

The National Dairy Council offers a number of excellent posters and charts that are useful for displays. For the local address, look under "Dairy Council" in your telephone book.

The National Education Association has a number of departments, each of which has various kinds of educational materials available. Write to: National Education Association, 1201 Sixteenth Street, N.W., Washington, D.C. 20036.

Government Agencies

Foreign Countries. Many countries offer posters and other colorful and informative materials through their embassies. Write to the specific embassy in Washington for information. Listed below are addresses of selected embassies.

Argentina, 1600 New Hampshire Ave., N.W., Washington, D.C.
Brazil, 3007 White Raven St., Washington, D.C.
Britain (for general information, write British Information Services, 45 Rockefeller Plaza, New York, N.Y.)
Canada, 1746 Massachusetts Ave., N.W., Washington, D.C.
Denmark, 2274 Massachusetts Ave., N.W. Washington, D.C.
France, 2535 Delmont Rd., N.W. Washington, D.C.
Germany, 1742 R. Street, N.W., Washington, D.C.
India, 2107 Massachusetts Ave., N.W., Washington D.C.
Japan, 2513 Massachusetts Ave., N.W. Washington, D.C.
Mexico, 2829 16th St., N.W., Washington, D.C.
Norway, 3401 Massachusetts Ave., N.W., Washington, D.C.
Spain, 2700 15th St., N.W., Washington, D.C.
Switzerland, 2900 Cathedral Ave., N.W., Washington, D.C.
Union of South Africa, 3101 Massachusetts Ave., N.W., Washington, D.C.
Yugoslavia, 1520 16th St., N.W., Washington, D.C.

State Agencies. You may wish to contact such state agencies as the State Promotion Office or the Division of Wildlife Resources for information on available materials. Check your telephone book under the name of your state for addresses and telephone numbers.

U.S. Department of Agriculture. Photographs, charts, maps, and posters are available for use in displays; you might also wish to consider the filmstrips, slides, and motion pictures that are distributed by this Department. Check your telephone book for the nearest local office.

U.S. Department of Commerce. Some excellent travel posters are available from this Department. Write to the Department of Commerce, Washington, D.C. 20230 for information.

U.S. Department of Transportation. A wide variety of materials, particularly on the subject of aviation, is available from this agency. Write to Special Assistant for Aviation Education, Office of General Aviation Affairs, Federal Aviation Administration, Washington, D.C. 20590.

U.S. Government Printing Office. This is the main source for most free and inexpensive materials. Many libraries maintain a file of GPO publications which you may wish to examine before placing an order. For a free price list of Government publications, write to the U.S. Government Printing Office, P.O. Box 1821, Washington, D.C. 20013. Be sure to specify your areas of interest.

Independent Sources

Bantam Books, Inc., 666 Fifth Avenue, New York, NY 10019 publishes a booklet entitled *1001 Valuable Things You Can Get Free,* that lists such free materials as posters, paintings, charts, etc., for use on display boards.

Dover Publications, 180 Varick Street, New York, NY 10014 publishes a low-priced guide entitled *Free and Inexpensive Education Aids* that contains sources for many display materials.

Educators Progress Service, Inc., 214 Center Street, Randolph, Wisconsin 53956 offers a series of guides to free materials.

Check your library for guides in your areas of interest. Those that include materials that are suitable for use in displays are as follows:

Fearon Publishers, 6 Davis Drive, Belmont, California 94002 publishes an inexpensive paperback that includes information on many materials that can be used in displays, titled *Selected Free Materials for Classroom Teachers.*

Field Enterprises Educational Corporation, Merchandise Mart Plaza, Chicago, Illinois 60654 provides a free list of special publications that includes many excellent items for use in displays.

Francis Press, P.O. Box 821, Greenwich Connecticut 06830 publishes an inexpensive catalog of sources for free materials.

The Office of Educational Services, George Peabody College for Teachers, Nashville, Tennessee 37203 offers an inexpensive catalog containing information on over 3,000 free items, including many maps, charts, posters, etc., that can be used on display boards.

Gordon Salisbury, P.O. Box 10751, Ventura, California 93001 publishes a catalog containing information on over one thousand free items, many of which are suitable for use in displays.

Dale E. Shaffer, 437 Jennings Ave., Salem, Ohio 44460 is a good source of information on free posters, charts, and maps. Write for the catalog on bulletin board items.

Appendix B

Color and Lettering in Displays

Letter Sizes

It is recommended that the minimum size of letters placed on the chalkboard be three inches. This rule applies when classrooms of average size are being utilized. A three-inch height may seem quite large, but this size is necessary due to the lack of contrast between the background (chalkboard surface) and the letter (formed with chalk on the surface). Also, the letter itself is not as nicely formed as is a pre-made or hand-made display letter.

For display letters, the following chart gives useful minimum sizes. These sizes are for lower case letters; capital or upper case letters should be made correspondingly larger.

Viewing distance	Minimum letter height
8 feet	¼ inch
16 feet	½ inch
32 feet	1 inch
64 feet	2 inches

Many teachers simply use a minimum letter size of one inch for display materials that are to be viewed by the total class. This is a safe approach to use.

The Use of Color in Displays

Color Psychology

The red-yellow family of colors is exciting, stimulating, happy. These are the "warm" colors, with red being the "hottest."

Red is associated with restlessness, agitation, aggressiveness, passion.

Yellow is associated with industriousness, energy, vitality.

The blue-green family of colors symbolizes the opposite emotions to the red-yellow group. These are described as being "cool." They are said to be leisurely and represent controlled emotions. Blue and green are popular colors that are associated with tenderness, peace, security, and calmness.

Blue is the coolest of the colors; although its connotations are for the most part positive, it is also related to sadness at times.

Green is related to life and growth. It is a logical favorite for springtime themes.

White is associated with lightness and airiness as well as with purity and solemnity.

Black is associated with death, sadness, and melancholy. But it can also be used in conjunction with themes of power and strength.

Color Combinations

The primary colors are used when maximum contrast is desired. The pairs are:

> red-green
> yellow-violet
> blue-orange

For value contrasts use combinations of light and dark colors, such as:

> white-black
> yellow-black
> yellow-dark blue, dark green
> white-dark blue, dark red, violet
> pastel colors, such as peach, pink, buff on dark colors, such as black, dark blue, violet

For brightness contrasts use a bright color with a dull one:

> red-white or light gray
> light red-black
> orange-gray blue
> red and orange-light blue, grays of lighter or darker value, black
> bright green-light gray, black
> bright blue-grayed brown

To emphasize important details use:

> red and orange (the "warm" advancing colors) to emphasize details
> blues, grayed green (the "cool" receding colors) as backgrounds or foils for the warm details

Appendix C

Display Evaluation

This evaluation sequence can be used to evaluate various kinds of displays, although the criteria will apply to a greater or lesser extent as the type of display changes. It is probably most useful where bulletin boards are being considered.

I. *Appropriateness.*
    A. Is the display appropriate to the stated purpose?
    B. Is the display appropriate to the audience? Factors that should be considered are:
        1. Past experience and readiness
        2. Age of individuals
        3. Socioeconomic background
        4. Ethnic origins

II. *Content.*
    A. Does the display have a definite theme?
    B. Is the information presented in an accurate and up-to-date manner?
    C. Is the information sufficient to meet the stated objectives? If not, will supplementary information be provided?
    D. Are verbal statements clear and concise? Is the vocabulary consistent with the capabilities of the audience?
    E. Is content pertinent and timely?

III. *Technical Quality.*
    A. Composition.
        1. Does the display seem to hold together? That is, does it have unity? Or, do the elements seem to be scattered about in a more or less random fashion?
        2. Is the color scheme appropriate to the concept? Or, does its use appear to be random, or even inappropriate?

      3. Does the display show contrast? Do the parts stand out one from another so that each is readily attended to?

      4. Is there a center of interest, or a point that is emphasized? This might be a title, or the main picture. A good display has one key element that sets the stage for the rest of the display.

  B. Lettering.

      1. Is the lettering of sufficient size and boldness to be clearly seen? Letter size can vary depending on how the display is to be used. If all parts are to be seen by a large group, then letters must be of considerable height and boldness. If the audience will have close access over a period of time, then smaller letters can be used.

      2. Are letters accurately spaced? A word should be readable without obvious breaks; also, letters shouldn't run together in a jumbled fashion.

      3. Is the letter style appropriate to the idea? Novelty letters would not be a good choice for a serious theme, but would be appropriate for a display on cartoon characters.

  C. Neatness.

      1. Are adhesives or fasteners hidden from view? Visible tacks, tape, etc., detract from the display.

      2. Are the elements carefully rendered, trimmed, outlined, etc.? Smudges, ragged edges, and random detail lines detract from the overall effect of the display.

      3. Are backgrounds neat, unobtrusive, and appropriate? Old bulletin boards and other types of backgrounds (notably colored papers) are often faded and full of tack holes; this can adversely affect an otherwise good display.

  D. Physical Considerations.

      1. Is the total display clearly visible to those who are expected to attend to it?

      2. Is the lighting adequate?

      3. Are the elements of sufficient size to be adequately seen by the group (if this is the strategy to be used)?

IV. *Utilization.*

  A. Were pupils involved in the construction of the display?

  B. During the utilization period, was the topic properly introduced?

C. During the utilization period, did pupils show an interest in the display?
D. During the utilization period, were pupils' questions encouraged and answered?

Rating Scale on the Utilization of Bulletin Boards

Below are statements describing the use of bulletin boards in classroom instruction. Circle the letter "R" for *regularly*, "O" for *occasionally*, and "N" for *never*, for whichever one of the three most nearly describes your use of your class bulletin board.

PRESENTATION

R O N   1. The bulletin board has a title.
R O N   2. Various sections of the bulletin board are labeled.
R O N   3. The available space is used economically.
R O N   4. The bulletin board is placed in the flow of traffic.
R O N   5. The material used is timely.
R O N   6. The bulletin board has a theme.
R O N   7. The material is well organized.
R O N   8. The board has the appearance of freshness.
R O N   9. Color is used in the displays.
R O N   10. The board is well lighted.
R O N   11. The board is readable.
R O N   12. Humor is used in materials.
R O N   13. The materials reflect the work of the class.
R O N   14. The materials are related to material being studied.
R O N   15. The board arouses interest.
R O N   16. The board teaches a lesson.
R O N   17. The board is not "windblown" in appearance.

ACTIVITIES

R O N   1. The bulletin board provides pupils opportunity for creative effort.
R O N   2. Pupils plan the use of the board.
R O N   3. Pupils collect bulletin board materials.
R O N   4. Pupils arrange and display materials.
R O N   5. Pupils file material to be kept.
R O N   6. Pupils make reports on bulletin board materials.
R O N   7. Pupils do supplementary reading on basis of bulletin board materials.
R O N   8. Pupils ask questions about display materials.
R O N   9. Pupils discuss bulletin board materials and their implications.
R O N   10. Pupils do group work in connection with bulletin board materials.
R O N   11. Pupils aid in the evaluation of effectiveness of the bulletin board in instruction.

SERVICES   The bulletin board is used for:

R O N 1. Announcements	R O N 7. Exhibits	
R O N 2. Assignments	R O N 8. Maps	
R O N 3. Cartoons	R O N 9. Flat pictures	
R O N 4. Charts	R O N 10. Illustrations of pupils' work	
R O N 5. Clippings		
R O N 6. Drawings	R O N 11. Magazine articles	
	R O N 12. Graphs	

Appendix D

Display Lettering Samples

ABCDE

FGHIJK

LMNOP

QRSTU

VWXYZ

A display alphabet that you can make yourself. Cut strips of paper that are five times as long as they are wide. Draw a square shape on a card that is the size of the letters that you wish to make. Position your strips of paper within the square, and move them around until they form letters that look like the ones above. Then, glue the strips together and trim the corners where needed (for example, B, C, D) to complete the letter.

ABCDEGHM

ABCDEHKM

Vinyl (top) and cardboard (bottom) letters that can be obtained from the Quik-Stik Company.

ABCDEFGHIMO

ABCDEGHMOP

ABCDEGSTUX

ABCDEGLMRSW

Dry-transfer or pressure-sensitive letters. The two top samples are from Letraset, the bottom two samples from Artype.

ABCDEFGHIJKL

ABCDEFGHIJKL

Display letters made with the Wrico system pens and guides (Wood-Regan Instrument Company).

ABCDEFG abcd

ABCDE abef

ABCDEFGHI

Display letters made with the Letterguide scriber and template system (Letterguide Co.).

SPECIAL TODAY

Display letters made with the Varigraph mechanical lettering system (Varigraph Co.).

GOD BLESS AMERICA

BEAUTIFUL

TWO FOUR

A selection of novelty letter forms made with the Stripprinter photographic lettering system (Stripprinter Inc.).

EDUCATIONAL

More ADVERTISING

MARKET PEOPLE

Examples of paper die-cut letters that are available from Stik-a-Letter Company.

About the Author

Robert V. Bullough, Sr., is Associate Professor in the Graduate School of Education, University of Utah. He holds a Ph.D. in Instructional Media and Administration, and a Master's degree in Painting and Sculpture. A practicing artist, he is represented in a number of private and public collections.

His teaching background includes 15 years as teacher and media coordinator (graphics) in the public schools, and 15 years as graphic supervisor and instructor in media at the university level.

Among his publications are two college texts on the production of teaching materials and several articles in such journals as *Educational Technology, Audiovisual Instruction,* and *Industrial Education.*

He currently teaches courses in graphic production, visual perception, visual literacy, and photography.